Emma

with Love for all your Kindness.

From

Betty - Joanne   Feb. 1998.

Strangford's Shores

Paintings by Alison Brown
Text by Jane E. M. Crosbie

Cottage Publications

First published by Cottage Publications,
Donaghadee, N. Ireland 1996.
Reprinted 1989
Copyrights Reserved.
© Illustrations by Alison Brown 1996.
© Text by Jane E. M. Crosbie1996.

Design and Orinination in N. Ireland
Printed in Singapore.

ISBN 1 900935 03 1

The Artist

Alison Brown has had an interest in art since her schooldays. Her talent blossomed in the 1980s under the guidance of painter James Watson on his out-door painting courses at Portaferry.

Alison draws her inspiration from the surrounding countryside, villages and buildings and her enjoyment of lighting and attention to detail is evident in her style. Her work has become much sought after and has won her a number of awards as well as being featured in several solo exhibitions.

In 1990 she set up Cottage Publications and published her first book of paintings and drawings on Donaghadee. Today she paints and runs the business with her husband Tim from their 200 year old cottage where they live with their three daughters Ruth, Clare and Rachel.

The Author

Jane E. M. Crosbie is an honours graduate in Modern History and Political Science from the Queen's University of Belfast.

She has specialised in the field of local historical studies, in particular early 20th century photographic collections.

A native of Bangor she is the author of 'A tour of North Down', 'A tour of the Ardes' and 'A tour of mid and south Down'. For several years she was an associate editor with Friar's Bush Press and is now a freelance editor and historical researcher.

Jane lives in Bangor with her husband and two cats.

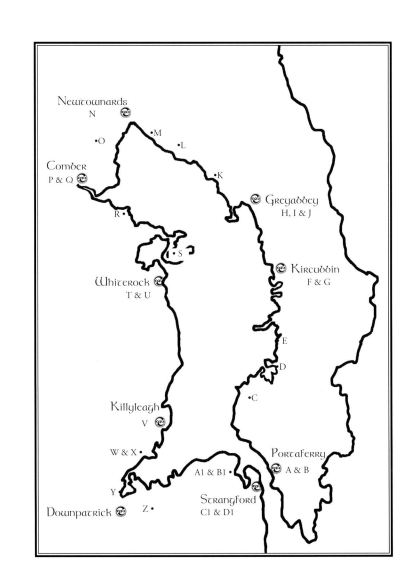

Contents

Beginnings

It is hard to believe that Strangford Lough was once situated on the equator. Of course, this was five hundred million years ago when the earth was still a young planet, but deposits laid down then and since have shaped the scenery we see and enjoy today.

The natural history of the Lough is as varied as the political and social. As the earth's crust moved and settled into the land masses with which we are familiar, each geographical age left behind its own imprint. For example the Caledonian period, during which the earth's crust was greatly distorted, left us with the narrow beds of rough slate from which generations of inhabitants derived their roofing.

The Lough is over thirty kilometres in length and sixty meters deep at some points. It is a haven for wildlife and is relatively sparsely populated which has resulted in our being able to enjoy much the same scenery as our forefathers. In his book *Strangford Lough: the Wildlife of an Irish Sea Lough* Robert Brown says that "No comparative area in Europe has such a range of habitats supporting such luxuriant life".

The Lough derives its name from the Vikings who, impressed or perhaps distressed by its vicious currents called it Strang-fiord, or turbulent lough. This was in marked contrast to the Irish name for it; Cuan – the quiet lough. The more romantic of us may say that even the Lough was reacting to those turbulent times.

Many of the layers of rocks laid down during the various geographical periods have been lost through erosion over the intervening millions of years. For example during the Carboniferous period both coal and limestone were developed. In Scotland, our nearest neighbour, the coal fields are extensive whereas in Ireland, with a few minor exceptions, any coal that there was has completely disappeared. Similarly with limestone in the Strangford area. We do know that it did exist as some remains at Castle Espie. It was extensively quarried in the nineteenth century and used both for building and agriculture. Limestone found elsewhere in the Lough was carried there by glaciers over 300 million years later.

Throughout the millions of years the land mass on which Ireland is located has risen and sunk back down again, and has gradually moved northwards to its present position. The climate has altered accordingly leaving behind some surprising fossils such as the footprints of an early form of dinosaur (possibly a Ticinosuchus or a Chirotherium) which lived around Scrabo during the Triassic period when the land was very arid and desert-like.

We still have evidence of this period in the red sandstone which was quarried from Scrabo hill and used to build the town hall in Newtownards and many other buildings such as the old Robinson and Cleaver department store in Belfast. The reddish tint was caused by the oxidisation of iron in the sand. This sandstone was created 225 million years ago.

It was not until the Tertiary period (a mere 65 million years ago) that the massive volcanic activity which characterised this period left us with many of our current landmarks, most notably Scrabo hill. The sandstone which makes up its core was permeated by molten lava which cooled and formed dolerite (a very hard rock similar to basalt). As the rest of the countryside was eroded by the combined effects of millions of years of weather and water, the dolerite protected the sandstone core of the hill. The climate at this time was quite a lot warmer than today and the rise in sea levels separated Ireland from Britain.

Not every geological age left its mark on the landscape of Strangford. This is not to say that the area was not affected but rather that what evidence may have existed has been eroded over the intervening millions of years. Thus we must make the gigantic leap from the Tertiary period which was 65 million years ago to the Quarternary, a mere 2 million years ago, to find the next layer of rocks. In *Strangford Lough* Robert Brown gives it the short description of "Blanket of glacial boulder clays, sands and gravels extending over most earlier rocks. Thinner in the south." However to the lay person it is perhaps better known as the Ice-Age.

What we know as the Ice-Age was not a continuous period of cold. There were many periods of relative warmth, some of which lasted for several thousands of years and which were a lot warmer than our weather today. Indeed there is a school of thought that says that we are merely enjoying one of those periodic warm periods and about a decade ago (before the dangers of global warming and holes in the ozone layer were discussed) some scientists were predicting a return to the Ice-Age.

Initally the start of the Ice-Age with the development of the great ice-caps on the higher mountain peaks and further north of Ireland had the converse effect of producing more arid conditions in the country. This resulted in the development of great grasslands and herbivores such as deer and horses flourished.

As the earth's climate continued to cool the ice caps began to spread down from the high mountains. The glaciers which affected much of the north of Ireland had their origin in the Highlands of Scotland and the damage that they caused to the existing landscape shaped the scenery we enjoy today. In Co. Antrim the glens were created by the ice eroding the basalt plateau as it did in Scotland itself. The glacier which had most effect on the Strangford Lough area originated in Lough Neagh and as such was a relative late comer.

When one thinks of glaciers one is inclined to imagine a huge block of clear ice. In reality the glacier contained much of the rubble it picked up as it slowly crept along the countryside: from bits of gravel and rotting vegetation to enormous boulders of bedrock gouged from the mountainsides. The effect of several thousand tons of ice and accumulated rubble on the countryside was quite dramatic. Only the harder forms of rock were able to withstand the enormous pressure, while the rest were either greatly distorted or swept along in its wake. On the countryside surrounding the lough the only areas which were able to withstand the worst effects of the ice were the hills of Craigantlet and of course Scrabo Hill.

It is possible to see the direction in which the glacier moved from the scars it left behind on the surface of the ground as it scraped its way slowly south-westwards. The crag and tail form of Scrabo shows this most dramatically with the large mound of sandstone and dolerite standing to the west and the tail sloping gently off to the east made up of the debris from the crag and other bits of accumulated rubble.

Perhaps the best known glacial feature left behind is the cluster of drumlins which are so characteristic of this area of Co. Down. Viewed from the air they look like the textbook description of a 'basket of eggs' and are found both totally on dry land or drowned to form the distinctive rounded islands that dot the Lough.

Drumlins were formed by boulder clay left behind by the glacier. They often have a rock core around which the clay accumulated and are usually an oval shape with gently sloping sides. Although the Lough's many islands are the most obvious examples, anyone who has driven from Strangford village to Downpatrick will have been able to enjoy the gently rolling landscape as the road snakes its way round the landlocked variety.

The ice gradually retreated about 12 000 years ago leaving in its wake the incongruous large boulders which are scattered on the shore. There are several large boulders on the shore-side of the road from Portaferry to Newtownards which were once caught up in the path of a glacier and left behind as the ice lost its strength. The end of the Ice-age was accompanied by a corresponding rise in the sea level. Evidence of this may be seen in the remanents of false beaches on the islands and shoreline of the Lough.

The end of the ice-age also signalled a return to the land of wildlife suited to a more temperate climate. During the Ice-age the land would have resembled the tundra of Greenland and Siberia today. It is quite possible that polar bears once stalked around Portaferry and Greyabbey. It is also possible that mammoths also roamed the area although no evidence has yet been found in Ulster. As the ice retreated the animals who had found refuge in the ice-free southern regions of Ireland gradually migrated northwards in search of fresh pastures. These included the giant Irish deer. A magnificent animal, the size of a clydesdale horse and with an antler span of three meters or almost ten feet, its remains have been found at Downpatrick, Portaferry and Scrabo.

The existence of herbivores encouraged hunters such as brown bears and wolves. The last of the wolves were killed at some stage during the 18th century, their only legacy being the beautiful Irish Wolfhounds. The raised sea levels which accompanied the big thaw finally isolated the island of Ireland from the rest of the British Isles. Thus the increase in the range of animals through migration was arrested in mid development. It is probably this reason, rather than any efforts of St. Patrick, which explains the absence of snakes from the island. It was still too cold for them to have come this far north. It also explains the absence of some other common wildlife such as moles, much to the delight of all gardeners in the land.

The northward migration of animals was preceded by the development of lush vegetation. There is evidence that the shores of the lough were covered with dense vegetation including forests of Oak, Elm, Willow and Hazel, all of which the first humans to venture into the country found very useful for food and shelter.

When one thinks of the history of the Strangford Lough one can be forgiven for only considering it in relation to man, but the actions of man were, until very recently, dictated by his natural habitat and that was shaped over five hundred million years ago. If we think of history as a 24 hour period man only arrived in Strangford at 23.58 and we are indeed fortunate that to a great extent we can still see the same landscape today as did the first arrivals.

Portaferry Castle was the home for generations of Savages. The Savage family arrived in the area with John de Courcy in the 12th century and it is they who shaped the town that we know today.

The old castle was built in the 16th century by Patrick Savage, Lord Savage of the little Ardes, who died in 1603. The castle was used as a residence until Portaferry House was built in 1821 and Arthur Young (the 18th century traveller, and author of Tour in Ireland, 1776-9) stayed there on 28 July 1776. The family changed its name to Nugent in 1797 and the change of name gave rise to a saying prevalent at the time "I'd rather have an old Savage than a new gent."

In the 17th century the Savages married into the Montgomery family and they benefited from an injection of money and business acumen to develop the town into a major port. Its heyday was in the 18th and 19th centuries when it was a thriving port with its own customs house. Much of the town centre and sea front that we see today dates from this period. However the advent of steam shipping, which required a deeper channel, sounded the death knell for the town as a port although the ferry continues to operate.

PORTAFERRY
WINDMILL HILL

With Thanks to Ards Borough Council

George Henry Bassett in his *County Down guide and directory of 1886* says that "Portaferry deserves to be classed among the most charmingly picturesque places in Ireland."

There has been a ferry service between the town and Strangford, just across the narrow entrance to the lough for centuries. It was mentioned by Walter Harris in 1744 in *The Ancient and Present State of the County of Down* when he noted that "a ferry-boat maintains a constant communication between the Baronies of Lecale and Ardes".

The town has long been an attractive destination for tourists. Whereas nowadays they are attracted by Exploris, the aquarium, in the past they were drawn by the rather more bizarre such as an arch made out of the jaw bones of a huge whale at Ballywhite which attracted visitors for over 150 years.

The town that we see today is remarkably unchanged by the passage of time. The best of the old has been preserved and visitors to the town are able to partake of such diverse activities as traditional music in the local bars, marine sports and study, locally run arts courses or simply enjoying the famous Ulster crack, all of which make Portaferry an increasingly popular holiday destination.

Portaferry
SHORE STREET

With Thanks to The Narrows

The countryside round Portaferry is littered with numerous old and picturesque houses. Some, like Marlfield, are old, traditionally built farmsteads and cottages, others are more substantial such as Portaferry House and Ballywhite House.

Portaferry House was built in 1821 for the Nugent/Savage family. It stands in beautiful parkland on the northern edge of the town. Ballywhite House was built in the 18th century and was improved and enlarged in 1870 for a Mr Warnock, a solicitor from Downpatrick. It was bought by a branch of the Brownlow family of Lurgan in 1918. The family owned extensive estates in Lurgan and Coolderry, Co. Monaghan. Major W. S. Brownlow tells of his great-uncle Charlie who on a trip back from Coolderry "was reputed to have driven the family car all the way up in 2nd gear because he was too frightened to change gear."

So little has the surrounding countryside changed since the opening decades of the 20th century that, when it was decided to make a film of Sam Hanna Bell's novel *The December Bride*, the film makers were able to film here where the author had originally set his book. Lisbane church which is featured in the film was built in 1777 during a flurry of building activity in the Ards peninsula in the second half of the 18th century. The Market House in Portaferry was restored in 1752 and the new Market House was built in Newtownards in 1771. It is testament to the skills of the craftsmen that all still stand today.

Portaferry

Marlfield

With Thanks to The Cornstore Restaurant

Stretching from the north of Portaferry to Ardkeen, this large nature reserve on the eastern shores of Strangford Lough has many interesting features. Marine plants and animals flourish in this unspoilt corner and one of the more unusual sights at the Dorn is a marine waterfall.

There is evidence on Castle Hill at Ardkeen of human habitation and worship stretching back to early Christian days. The first earthen fortress was constructed by the original inhabitants and the church had its origins at the same time.

It was here that William, Baron le Savage (the first of the family to arrive in the area) chose to construct his castle c.1180. The position gave him an uninterrupted view of the area and enabled him to establish a control over the peninsula that the family maintained over the following centuries.

The old castle was demolished in the early 17th century and the stones used to build a new house to the west of the hill. This house was pulled down in its turn and the stones used to build the farmhouse which is still there.

Similarly the church was recycled over the centuries. The original church was the Church of St. Mary which dated from the pre-Anglo-Norman period. This was rebuilt by the Savages in the intervening years and was later adopted by the Church of Ireland. It has been in ruins for over 100 years and Robert Lloyd Praegar writing at the beginning of the 20th century said that "Now, the silence of the ruins is broken only by the lowing of the cattle and the scream of the sea-birds".

Ardkeen

CASTLE HILL, ARDKEEN

The Saltwater Brig marks the divide between the Upper and Lower Ards. It was once an island, only connected with the rest of the peninsula by the two bridges which still remain.

The present bar at Saltwater Brig is thought to date from c.1793, but there must have been a building here before that as after 1765 it became an offense to erect a house within 25 feet of a rural road. The local landlords were the Savage family and in November 1810 a lease was issued to a John McGrath for one life and twenty-one years for Saltwater Brig and several farms in the area, total yearly rent £34 3s. The lease includes the provision to exchange 4 days work on the landlords estate for 4s 4d and also 4 fat hens for the same amount. This gives a good indication of the value of a day's labour.

The house has been a public house for at least two centuries although in 1838 the rent statement records that it was an "old dilapidated concern not worth £5." Despite this the landlord added 4s 6d to the rent for "good situation".

In the present century the bar only opened for one day a year, All Saints Day, until the 1970s. Lisbane Church, which is just next door, still only opens on All Saints Day each year and the key to the church is kept behind the bar. Film buffs may recognise the church (which dates from 1777) as it featured in the film of Sam Hanna Bell's book *December Bride*.

Ardkeen

Saltwater Brig

With Thanks to The Saltwater Brig Inn

Kircubbin is a relative newcomer to the area as Samuel Lewis explains in the *Topographical dictionary of Ireland* in 1846 "This town is of very recent origin, having been built since the year 1790, previously to which time there were not more than five houses in the place."

The town and harbour were owned by the Ward family of Bangor Castle and they developed the harbour in the early 19th century. Given the awful state of the roads in the Ards peninsula it was often easier to transport goods by sea to a convenient harbour. Bassett recorded the import of coal, salt and Indian corn and the export of grains, beans and potatoes from the harbour. Another export which brought with it great prosperity was that of Kelp which was collected in vast quantities and exported to Liverpool. Kelp was much used as a fertiliser before the advent of the man-made variety.

Another industry which flourished was linen and there was a brown linen hall in the town where local weavers were able to sell their unbleached linen. Until quite recently women in the peninsula were able to augment the family's income by finishing pieces of linen and every town and village had its own linen agent. One resident of the area remembers from the 1930s the women rushing to see the agent in an attempt to get 'Initialling' which was better paid than embroidering flowers.

Another source of employment in the mid-19th century was the manufacture of straw hats and bonnets although this had died out by the end of the century, no doubt hit as much by inclement weather as by more mechanised forms of manufacturing.

Kircubbin

KIRCUBBIN HARBOUR

With Thanks to Charles Gilmore Galleries, Holywood

Strangford Lough from earliest times was essential in the prosperity of the many towns and villages which are scattered along its shores. Until surprisingly late in the present century communications, especially along the Ards peninsula, were very bad and many farmers found it both quicker and easier to transport their produce and farm animals by boat than by road. However this was not always as safe as it might at first appear and on several occasions the boats fell victim to the treacherous currents and strong tides in the Lough.

Even people who were brought up on the Lough and used it every day have fallen victim to it in the past. In January 1903 two local men, John Williamson and his son Robert, had piloted a steamer from Portaferry to Killyleagh when, on their way home, the boat was blown onto Jackdaw Island and they both died of exposure.

Not all the trade which was conducted in the Strangford Lough was strictly legal. In the 18th century one particular trade which was greatly discouraged by the authorities was smuggling. Unfortunately for the authorities as a result of prohibitive import duties smuggling was not regarded as a proper crime by the local population and there were dark mutterings that some government officials were not above dabbling in it themselves.

Kircubbin

Yachts at Kircubbin

With Thanks to McGimpsey & Kane (Builders)

The village of Greyabbey may look like a sleepy, picturesque place today, but 200 years ago it was a hotbed of unrest and dissent. Many of its inhabitants were involved in the United Irishmen rebellion of 1798, fighting on both sides and the Presbyterian Minister was executed for his involvement with the rebels.

The Rev. James Porter was a well-known radical minister who had regularly contributed to the *Northern Star,* a newspaper owned by Samuel Neilson. Political power at this time rested solely with the members of the established Church of Ireland. The Presbyterian community of the north of Ireland had been inspired by the activities of both the French revolution and, more importantly, by their fellow kinsmen in the American colonies to agitate for political reform.

At his trial Rev. Porter was accused of treasonable acts, namely that he had been with a body of insurgents. Despite witnesses for the defence who said that he had merely been talking to them, he was found guilty of treason and sentenced to death.

His execution was posthumously recorded by his son James (the attorney-general for Louisiana), who recounted that "On the morning of the day which terminated my father's life (2 July 1798) he...was conducted under a guard of cavalry from Newtownards to Greyabbey. A temporary gallows was erected on a small hill which overlooked the meeting-house where he had officiated as pastor for ten years. My mother rode with him to the place of execution. They arrived at the fatal spot, my mother kissed him for the last time...she returned to the manse...In an hour after, the body...was delivered to her a corpse."

Greyabbey
GREYABBEY VILLAGE

With Thanks to Rara Avis

Writing in 1886 W. G. Bassett described Greyabbey as "one of the handsomest villages in the county". If he were to return today it is doubtful if he would change his opinion.

The Grey Abbey, which is thought to have got its name from the colour of the monks robes, dates from 1193 when it was founded by Affreca, who was the daughter of the King of Man and wife of John de Courcy. The monastery was run by the Cistercian order and survived until 1541 when it fell victim to the dissolution of the monasteries and its lands were seized by the crown. In 1572 it was burnt by Sir Brian MacPhelim O'Neill to prevent it being used by English troops during an ill-fated attempt at settlement.

The abbey and its lands were part of the estate given to the Montgomery family in the early 17th century by Con O'Neill of Clanaboye. Sir Hugh Montgomery restored part of the nave of the abbey as a church and it was used until 1778. Most of the family are buried inside the ruined church. The Montgomerys did not enjoy uninterrupted occupation of the village as in 1652 the estate was forfeited by Cromwell and given to Colonel Robert Barrow the commander of the Northern force. The family recovered their estate after the Restoration and have owned Greyabbey ever since, although they sold Newtownards and Comber to Sir Robert Colville in 1675 and the towns were bought by the Stewarts (of Mount Stewart) in the 1740s.

Greyabbey
GREY ABBEY

With Thanks to Traders at Hoops Courtyard

One of the more remarkable stories to emerge from the turbulent times of 1798 was that of David Bailie Warden.

Warden was a schoolteacher and in training for the Presbyterian ministry when he became involved in the United Irishmen rebellion. He tried to raise the populations of Bangor and Donaghadee, but only succeeded in assembling a group of about 300 men whom he led to Movilla on the outskirts of Newtownards.

Lord Castlereagh, the local landlord and prominent politician, personally led the hunt for Warden through the numerous islands of Strangford Lough. Warden was eventually deported to the American colonies. It was here that the story took an unusual turn. He became an American citizen in 1804 and returned to Europe as the private secretary to the American minister in Paris. In 1808 he was authorised to act as American consul *pro tempore*.

In 1815 the United States was invited to send observers to the Congress of Vienna, which followed the end of the Napoleonic war. It was here that Warden, now a respectable diplomat, came face to face with Castlereagh his former enemy.

Visitors to Mount Stewart may still see the chairs from the Congress of Vienna in the dining room.

Greyabbey

MID ISLAND

With Thanks to Marilyn Dixon, Peninsula Equestrian Academy

Mount Stewart House was the family home of the Marquis of Londonderry. The house dates from the 18th century although it was greatly remodelled in the 19th century and what we see today is much changed from the original home of Lord Castlereagh.

Although the house has many attractions the estate is best known for the famous gardens which were the creation of Edith, 7th Marchioness of Londonderry who laid them out in the 1920s. The first garden to be started was the Sunken garden, which was financed by the proceeds from their horse Polemake winning the St Leger.

From the Sunken garden, steps lead the visitor out to the Shamrock garden with its Irish motif, complete with a floral red hand of Ulster. To the south-west of the House is the Italian Garden which leads into the Spanish garden and finally the Mairi Garden which is in the shape of a Tudor rose. The theme for the garden is the nursery rhyme *Mary, Mary, quite contrary* and it was here that Lady Mairi Bury (Edith's daughter) was placed in her pram while a child. The gardens contain many exotic plants from the four corners of the earth but one of the most beautiful sites is the carpet of bluebells on the edges of the drive down to the front of the house which bloom every spring.

Edith, Lady Londonderry, was a great political hostess and she and her husband entertained a great many political friends at both Mount Stewart and their home, Londonderry House, in London. They were members of the Ark Club, an elite group of politicians and officers during the first world war. All the members had nicknames, Edith was Circe the Sorceress, Winston Churchill was Winston the Warlock and Arthur Balfour was Albert the Albatross. The Londonderrys had a very varied circle of friends and acquaintances and both Ramsey MacDonald, the first Labour Prime Minister and Baron von Ribbontrop the Nazi Ambassador to London were guests in their homes.

Mount Stewart

MOUNT STEWART HOUSE & GARDENS

With Thanks to The National Trust

Cunningburn Mill is situated slightly inland between Greyabbey and Newtownards. The compilers of *Place-names of Northern Ireland volume two* say that "This name appears to have been coined in the variety of English spoken by Scottish and English settlers at an early stage in the plantation of North Down. It is likely that it was named after the nearby stream known as Cunning Burn."

The present buildings, which were listed in the late 1950s, comprise a watermill and drying kiln which are dated 1776 and a flax mill from c.1886. The cottage predates the watermill and kiln. After the big wind of 1839 the *Northern Whig* reported that "In the wide district of Ards scarcely a corn or flax mill has escaped, except Cunningburn Mill and Mr Bailie's of Greyabbey."

The Warden family (who are related to David Bailie Warden) has owned the mill for over 100 years. They worked the mill until the early 1930s when the coming of electricity to the peninsula signalled the beginning of the end of its working life. Prior to the advent of electricity all the farmers in the area would bring their grain to the mill to be ground. Afterwards they could mill their own grain in small electrical grinders. The irony is that it took several years for Cunningburn Mill itself to be connected with electricity. The drainage scheme at Movilla during the Second World War resulted in the end of the mill's working life as it took the water from the mill pond.

Cunningburn

CUNNINGBURN MILL

With Thanks to Sheldon Gallery

The shores of Strangford have been home over the centuries to numerous fighting men and women but perhaps none were as famous or renowned as Lieutenant Colonel Robert Blair Mayne D.S.O. (and three bars).

Blair Mayne was born in Newtownards in 1915 and attended the local Regent House School. He graduated in law from the Queen's University of Belfast and was a distinguished rugby player, winning six international caps and toured South Africa with the British Lions in 1938. But for the intervention of the Second World War he would have continued his legal career as a Belfast solicitor. Instead he joined up in 1939 and so embarked on an extraordinary military career during which he won the Distinguished Service Order four times and rose to the rank of Chief of the Special Air Service.

He was one of the founding members of the S.A.S. and was active in the war in North Africa. In one raid alone he personally destroyed 47 enemy planes. Later he was in command of the unit which opened the assault on Sicily and it was during the war in Italy that he and his unit captured an Italian train (behind enemy lines) and drove it into a concentration camp. There they captured the guards, released the prisoners and brought the entire group (including the Colonel Commandant) by train back to Allied control. During the war in France he parachuted behind German lines and successfully disorganised the German retreat after the American breakthrough by wrecking over 1,000 trucks.

After the war he embarked on an Antarctic expedition but was forced to retire in February 1946 because of a back injury sustained during the war. On his return he became the Secretary of the Incorporated Law Society of Northern Ireland.

He was killed in a car accident in Newtownards in the early hours of Wednesday, 14 December 1955 when his car hit a parked lorry in Mill Street. His funeral, held on Friday, 16 December was attended by thousands and two hearses were required to carry all the floral tributes.

In the obituary which appeared in the *Spectator* his friend H. Malcolm McKee, M.C. said of him that he was "Probably the most gallant man and toughest fighter Northern Ireland gave to the Second War. A Son of Ards we are all proud of."

Newtownards

SCRABO FROM THE PORTAFERRY ROAD

With Thanks to Page 1 Books & News

The 'New town' of Ards was established in the 12th century when a village grew up around a castle which had been erected by the Anglo-Normans. When the Montgomery family arrived in the 17th century the area had been devastated by Sir Brian Phelim O'Neill and according to the *Montgomery Manuscript* "30 cabins could not be found, nor any stone walls, but ruined roofless churches... and a stump of an old castle in Newtown, in each of which some Gentlemen sheltered themselves at their first coming over".

In the 19th century Newtownards was the third largest town in Co. Down after Newry and Downpatrick and was the main market town in the area for farm produce. It was a centre of linen production and people moved into the town from the neighbouring countryside to seek employment. The population grew from 4 442 in 1831 to 10 149 in 1926.

The original Market house in Newtownards was beside the Market Cross at the junction of Movilla Street, High Street and Church Street. It was replaced in 1771 with the present building in Conway Square. This is now the Town Hall and home to the Ards Arts Centre. Sir Charles Brett, in *Ulster Court and Market Houses* describes it as the finest market house in the Province. There is a link with its original purpose each Saturday when the market is held in the square.

Newtownards

THE SQUARE AND MARKET HOUSE

With Thanks to Ards Borough Council

The Londonderry Monument, or Scrabo Tower as it is perhaps better known, was built in 1859 in memory of General Charles William Vane-Stewart, the 3rd Marquis of Londonderry.

The fighting Marquis, as he was known, had a very colourful career. He was a Lieutenant Colonel of the 5th Dragoons when the regiment was disbanded for insubordination. During the Peninsula War he was Adjutant-General to Sir Arthur Wellesley, later Duke of Wellington and later was ambassador to Vienna.

Like his contemporary, Rollo Gillespie from Comber, he fought a duel. In his case it was with Henry Grattan, leader of the Patriot Party and neither was seriously injured. In later life he wielded the pen rather than the sword and wrote an eight volume *Life of Lord Castlereagh* (his ancestor) as well as a *Narrative of the Peninsular War.* He appeared in print himself as Col. von Trumpetson in Disraeli's novel, *Vivian Grey.*

The tower is a prominent landmark sitting as it does on a crag and tail, left behind after the Ice age. The hill is also home to one of the most unusual golf courses in Ireland. Scrabo Golf Club was founded on 13th December 1907 and Blair Mayne who lived close by was one of the more famous past members.

Newtownards

SCRABO TOWER

With Thanks to In–Sport

The Gillespie Monument in the middle of the town square in Comber is dedicated to the memory of Major-General Sir Robert Rollo Gillespie, K.C.B.

Had the Major-General's life story been made into a film, the lead role would have been played by either Errol Flynn or Clarke Gable. He was a military hero of the true romantic, swashbuckling genre.

Born in Comber in 1766 he joined the 3rd Irish Horse at the age of seventeen. At the age of twenty he eloped with Miss Annabell Taylor after a whirlwind romance of three weeks. He fought a duel with, and killed, the brother of Sir Jonah Barrington. At his subsequent trial the jury returned a verdict of not guilty of wilful murder, going against the instructions of the presiding judge.

On his way to the West Indies in 1792 he was ship-wrecked but managed to escape with a few companions in an open boat. While in the West Indies he fought off a band of eight bandits single-handed. Armed only with a sword he killed six of his attackers and the other two took flight.

By 1806 he was in India, where he distinguished himself during a mutiny of Sepoy troops. In 1811 he led an expedition into Java, returning to India in 1812.

His death in 1814 was as romantic as his life. He fell fatally wounded leading the Meerut division of the Bengal troops in an attack on the fort of Kalunga in the Himalayas during the Nepal war. He died a hero's death. Sword in hand and shot through the heart his last words were reputed to be "One shot more for the honour of Down!"

Comber

COMBER SQUARE

With Thanks to Ards Borough Council

The Andrews family has long been associated with Comber. As far back as 1779 John Andrews raised and commanded a company of Volunteers from the town. In the 1850s John Andrews, the High Sheriff of Down founded John Andrews and Co. Linen Mill which has provided employment and housing for the people of the town for over 150 years.

However perhaps the most renowned member of the family was Thomas Andrews who was born on 7th February 1873. Nicknamed the 'Admiral' by family and friends because of his fondness for boats, he entered Harland and Wolff as a premium apprentice on 1st May 1889 at the age of sixteen. By 1905 he had risen to the position of Chief Designer and as such he was responsible for the design of many of the great boats produced by the shipyard during its zenith. The most famous of these was the Titanic.

When the Titanic left Belfast on 2nd April 1912 to finish her sea trials Thomas Andrews was on board, as he had been on many of the other great liners he had designed. He was also on board when she left the port of Southampton at 12 noon on 10th April with over 2,200 passengers and crew.

At 11.40 p.m. ships time on Sunday 14th April 1912 the Titanic collided with an iceberg. At first Andrews went below decks to inspect the damage, then realising the seriousness of the situation he calmly went round the boat helping to supervise the evacuation. Surviving officers said that his calmness helped to ensure that as many people as possible were rescued. A few minutes before the end witnesses saw him on the Boat deck throwing deck chairs overboard to the people struggling in the water.

In a cable dated New York, 19th April 1912 it said "Interview Titanic's officers. All unanimous Andrews heroic unto death, thinking only safety others." He went down with the ship he had designed and of which he was so proud.

Comber

ANDREWS MILL

With Thanks to Spratt Insurance

Castle Espie is one of only three sites of Carboniferous rocks to be seen in County Down. The limestone was much excavated in the 19th century and it is still possible to see the disued lime kiln.

The area has been occupied from earliest days and the lime kiln is not the only reminder of past inhabitants. A mile or so outside Castle Espie are the remains of a cromlech, an ancient grave and, a little further away, the remains of a stone circle. The five large stones which remain are called the five sisters.

The most numerous of the present day inhabitants are the various birds and butterflies of the Wildfowl and Wetlands Trust Visitor Centre. There are a over 50 different kinds of birds in residence throughout the year from migratory visitors such as the Brent Geese to the resident ducks. It is possible to feed some of the more adventurous of the birds by hand.

The area is also a haven for traditional local wild flowers which are discouraged in other more cultivated areas. On a nice day it is possible to wander through the area and observe a habitat which has not changed in centuries.

Comber

CASTLE ESPIE

With Thanks to The Old Schoolhouse Inn, Comber

Nendrum was one of a series of important ecclesiastical sites which flourished in Ireland in the so-called Dark Ages. Monks from this establishment together with those from nearby Movilla and Bangor, kept the art of religious study alive at a time when the rest of Europe was being overrun by paganism.

The monastery was founded c.450 by St. Mochaoi, who had been converted by St. Patrick, and past pupils included St. Caylan the first Bishop of Down and St. Finnian of Movilla. Despite being attacked in 974 by the Vikings the monastery survived as a place of worship and was later well endowed by John de Courcy.

Writing in 1900 Robert Lloyd Praegar in his *Official Guide to the County Down and the Mountains of Mourne* was still able to report that "At its Mahee Islande western end ... are the obscure remains of the ancient ecclesiastical colony of Nendrum". It was not until the 1920s that the site was excavated by the the Belfast Natural History and Philosophical Society.

Several interesting artifacts were discovered. Amongst them was the Bell of Nendrum (which may now be seen in the Ulster Museum) and a sundial which was put into the remaining wall of the church. This sundial is one of only three such dials existing in Ulster the others being found in Bangor and Clogher. It does not record the hours of the day as is conventional, but rather records the ecclesiastical hours for matins, vespers etc.

Mahee

NENDRUM MONASTIC SITE

With Thanks to Andrew Noble D.C.

The shores of Strangford are littered by reminders of distant times as well as the more recent past. Examples of early Irish settlements rest alongside those of the monastic era and the middle-ages.

Sketrick castle is a remnant of the Anglo-Norman conquest of Ireland. This conquest was achieved during the reign of King John (of Robin Hood fame) and was limited to the eastern shores of the island of Ireland. Sketrick was one of twenty seven such fortresses built along the shores of Strangford Lough.

It is thought to have been built by the de Mandevilles who had first arrived with King John in 1210 to help him defeat a rebellion by de Courcy (who had originally conquered the area) and as a reward were given manors in Comber, Killyleagh, Groomsport and Castle Ward. However the first mention of the castle is in 1470 when it was captured by the Clanaboye O'Neills. The castle stood derelict for many centuries until 1896 when the south-western corner fell down. To date it has resisted the temptation for complete destruction and remains an interesting landmark.

Whiterock

SKETRICK ISLAND AND CASTLE

With Thanks to Ards Borough Council

When one wanders round the islands that scatter the shores of Strangford around Killinchy and Killyleagh the connection with the stylish Sloane Square is not immediately obvious. However Killyleagh was the birthplace of Sir Hans Sloane the naturalist and physician, founder of the British Museum and the person after whom Sloane Square, Sloane Street and the exclusive Hans Place are named.

He was born in Killyleagh in 1666 and spent his formative years in the area. No doubt the beautiful countryside around Killyleagh and Killinchy fostered his great love of nature and one can imagine him exploring the many island in the Lough.

Hans Sloane studied medicine in the University of Orange in south-east France and qualified in 1683. He went to the West Indies as Physician to the Duke of Albemarle, Governor of Jamaica and it was here that he started his large botanical collection. He returned to London in 1689 and started up his medical practice. He was Secretary of the Royal Society from 1693 to 1712 and in 1698 he published a catalogue of Jamaican plants followed in 1707 and 1725 with two volumes of his travels.

In 1716 he was made a baronet and in 1727 was elected President of the Royal Society, a position which he held until 1741. His eldest daughter married the 2nd Lord Cadogan who owned the area of London which now bear both their names. Hans Sloane died in 1753 and he bequeathed his entire collections to the nation on condition of a payment of £20 000 to his family. This was a fraction of what it had cost him to collect. An Act of Parliament in 1753 accepted the offer and the collection formed the nucleus of what became the British Museum.

Killinchy

ISLANDS FROM KILLINCHY

There has been a castle in Killyleagh since the 13th century. The first was built by the de Mandeville family and ownership was passed to the Whytes. The castle was awarded to the Hamilton family by James I (& VI) in 1610 and they have retained possession ever since apart from briefly losing control of it to the Cromwellians in 1649. This makes Killyleagh castle the oldest continuously occupied castle in Ireland.

The grandson of James Hamilton, Henry Hamilton, 2nd Earl of Clanbrassil was responsible, indirectly for a curious situation whereby the castle and the gatehouse were owned by different branches of the one family. He married the daughter of the Earl of Drogheda who (in the words of Lt. Col. D.A. Rowan Hamilton in his article *The Hamiltons of Killyleagh*) "turned out to be a right old bag. He was impotent and I would think rather weak in the head."

Henry made a will, against the advice of his family, leaving everything to his wife who then poisoned him. The will was contested and after a long drawn out legal battle which lasted from his death in 1675 to c.1700 the estate was divided with a nephew getting the castle and a niece getting the gatehouse. 162 years later the estate was reunited when the eldest son of the gatehouse family (who were the Blackwoods, ie the Dufferins of Clandeboye) married the eldest daughter of the castle thus reuniting the two families.

The family name was changed from Hamilton to Rowan Hamilton by Archibald Hamilton who effected the change to inherit a large fortune from his maternal grandparents. He was a wild character who became involved in the United Irishmen and was sentenced to death. Imprisoned in Dublin Castle he persuaded his guard to let him visit his wife in their Dublin home. With the guard sitting outside the bedroom door, Archibald escaped via a rope from the bedroom window and fled the country. He was later pardoned and died in the castle.

Killyleagh
KILLYLEAGH CASTLE

With Thanks to Sloane's Emporium

Situated between Downpatrick and Killyleagh on the shore of the Lough is Delamont Country Park. The estate is comprised of over 200 acres of woodland and meadows.

There is evidence on the estate of human habitation for over 1000 years: from the early Christian rath or 'fairy fort' to Delamont House. The house is now the property of the Belfast Education and Library Board but was the home of the Gordon family for many years.

Delamont was acquired in the early 19th century by David Gordon JP who was married to the youngest daughter of James Crawford of Crawfordsburn. He already owned Florida Manor in Ballygowan which had been a wedding gift from his father in-law. It would appear that he bought Delamont as a home for his second son Rev. James Crawford Gordon while his eldest son Robert inherited Florida Manor. However Robert died without issue in 1864 and the two estates were merged. James also died without children and the estates passed to a cousin, who also had no children so the properties were divided between two nephews. Again one died without children and the properties were reunited and passed, at the beginning of the century to Alexander Hamilton Miller Haven Gordon.

The country park is a haven for wildlife with one of the largest heronries in Ireland. There is a large bird-hide in the grounds and it is possible to see a wide range of wildlife such as Kestrel, Sparrowhawk, Guillemots and Curlews as well as aquatic mammals such as otters and seals.

Killyleagh
BARN AT DELAMONT

With Thanks to The Smuggler's Table

The shores of Strangford Lough are home to numerous yacht clubs. The one at Quoile was founded after the Second World War. It was originally located on the river Quoile but moved to its present location on the estuary after the new tidal barrier was built at Hares Island in 1957.

The Quoile Yacht Club is, in common with the others on the lough, a friendly club which attracts a large number of sailing enthusiasts from both the local area and further afield. It has a big large-handicap yacht class and a large fleet of Enterprise dinghies. Although there are the usual sailing nights and races many people enjoy just pottering around the many islands which litter the lough. Nothing nicer on a warm summers day.

Nearby Gibbs Island which is just to the south of the Delamont Estate is one such destination. A small island which is densely wooded it is accessible by both sea and land. It is referred to locally as the Royal Island as Charles, Prince of Wales, spent many happy days playing here when a child.

Killyleagh

GIBBS ISLAND AND QUOILE FROM DELAMONT

With Thanks to Down District Council

The Quoile Pondage is essentially a man-made feature. It was created when a tidal barrier was built on the Quoile estuary at Hare Island in 1957 to help alleviate the problem of flooding in Downpatrick.

The Quoile estuary was important to Downpatrick as it linked the town and its hinterland with Strangford Lough. In 1717 Quoile Quay was built and a busy port developed which operated for over two centuries with corn, linen and hides being exported aided by the extension of the railway to Downpatrick in the 19th century.

In 1686 a stone bridge was built across the Quoile and at the Downpatrick end there was a toll-gate which was abolished in 1744. At the Saltwater Bridge on the Killyleagh Road there was a tide-mill whose miller lived in the large house beside the mill.

Flooding had always been a problem in the area and the floodgates or tidal barrier built in 1957 were not the first such structure to be built. Floodgates were built, close to the Quoile Bridge in 1745 and again in 1802 and 1934. However they failed to cure the problem and the new barriers were erected. The pondage comprises 450 acres of freshwater wetland as opposed to saltwater and one of the side effects has been the gradual development of new flora and fauna in the area. There is a nature reserve and information centre for the area.

Downpatrick
QUOILE BRIDGE

With Thanks to Hugh Press, Alexander, Reid & Frazer

According to tradition it was here that St. Patrick started his mission to Ireland and here also that he died in 461.

The Church of Ireland church is thought to be on the site of the original barn where Patrick founded his first church in 462. This was given to him by Dichu, the local chieftain and his first convert. Saul is the English version of the Irish word Sabhall, meaning barn. Nothing remains of either the first church or the later Augustinian monastery which flourished here in the early Christian period. It was too close to Strangford and it never recovered from frequent raids by the Vikings.

The monastery was revived in the 12th century by the Bishop of Down, Malachy O Morgair, and briefly regained some of its earlier importance under the patronage of Anglo-Normans. The dissolution of the monasteries in the 16th century led to another lean period and no church was maintained on the site until it was adopted by the Church of Ireland in 1788. The present church was erected in 1932 to commemorate the 1500th anniversary of St. Patrick's arrival.

The whole area is littered with holy wells. They were originally pagan in origin but were quickly adopted by the new Christian religion. Two miles away from Saul are the ruins of one of the oldest churches in Ireland, Raholp. It was dedicated to St. Tassach, the Bishop who gave the dying Patrick his last communion.

Downpatrick
SAUL CHURCH

With Thanks to Down District Council

Audley's Castle is situated on a rocky outcrop about a mile north-west of Strangford. It was built in the 15th century by the Audley family who leased the estate from the local landowner the Earls of Kildare.

The Audleys, like many other Anglo-Norman settlers, became so integrated with the locals that they became "more Irish than the Irish". They joined with other members of the Catholic gentry in Rebellion in 1641 and as a result they forfeited their estates. The estate passed back into the hands of the Earls of Kildare who later sold it to Robert Ward of Castle Ward. John Magee in *A Journey through Lecale* notes that "The first floor room has been restored, with a fireplace, windows and cupboards, and nowhere is it easier to imagine the life-style of the occupiers of towerhouses in the fifteenth and sixteenth centuries".

Audley's Castle is one of many such towerhouses in the area. One of the most notable is Walshestown Castle about 4 miles from Downpatrick. It was built by the Walshe family who arrived in the area with de Courcy. In the 17th century it was given to the Anderson family who modernised it and continued to live there until the 19th century.

Strangford

Audley's Castle

With Thanks to The Harlequin / The Bridge Gallery

Castle Ward House sits on the western shore of Strangford Lough, just a few miles outside the town of Strangford. The Ward family have owned the estate since they bought it from the Earl of Kildare in 1570. They built a tower-house where they continued to live until the 18th century.

In the early 18th century Michael Ward, the M.P. for County Down married Anne Hamilton of Bangor Castle whose Bangor estates they inherited. They built a large house of which nothing now remains.

Bernard, 1st Viscount Bangor (the son of Michael and Anne) inherited the estate in 1759. He was married to Lady Anne Blith the daughter of the 1st Earl of Darnley. It is thanks to this couple that the wonderfully eccentric house which we enjoy today was built.

Mary, Mrs Delany, wife of the Dean of Down and the great letter writer, was a visitor to Castle Ward while the new building was being discussed. On 12th July 1760 she wrote that "We went to Castle Ward on Wednesday...It is altogether one of the finest places I ever saw." However three years later she was voicing her concerns in a letter to her brother Bernard Granville, dated 29 August 1763 "Mr Ward is building a fine house...He wants taste and Lady Anne Ward is so whimsical that I doubt her judgement. If they do not do too much they can't spoil the place, for it hath every advantage from Nature that can be desired."

Mrs Delany need not have worried. The couple could not agree on an overall theme for the house. He favoured the classical style in vogue at the time, she was consumed with the romance of the Gothic style of architecture. So they agreed to differ and the house is divided into two, each half reflecting the style of its author. It is an absolute delight of a house.

Strangford

CASTLE WARD HOUSE

With Thanks to The National Trust

Strangford is thought to have been founded by the Vikings who used it as a base from which to raid monasteries and settlements. Nothing remains of their stay other than the name of both town and lough.

The sheltered harbour at Strangford has been its best asset through the years and by 1514, when it and Ardglass were granted to the Earls of Kildare by Henry VIII, there was already a thriving port in the town. In the early 17th century the harbour and town were developed by the agent of the Earl, Valentine Payne, who wrote in 1629 "I have ... builded a key where there was none before, that the biggest shippe the king hathe may lay her side by it. Besides I have builded a custom house".

Strangford became the main port for Downpatrick and by the end of the 18th century it was the eighth biggest port in Ireland. Unfortunately the fact that the railway did not extend to Strangford, along with the development of steam shipping, which required deeper harbours, led to its gradual decline throughout the late 19th century.

Strangford House was built by the Collector of Customs, Collector Norris in the early 18th century. This led to many raised eyebrows as he would not have earned enough to pay for such an impressive structure and rumours persisted of how the very close friendships between him and some local merchants resulted in the customs collected never seeming to tally with the amount of goods landed.

Strangford

STRANGFORD VILLAGE

With Thanks to Johnson's Coffee

And so we reach the end of our trip round the Lough. It is fortunate that the area has been little altered by the years and has for the most part escaped the more distressing features of modern development.

On the way the many characters that the lough produced have sought to make themselves known. It is amazing that such a relatively small area should have produced so many notable people. Perhaps there is something in the air that inspires one to greatness.

The many islands and twisting coastline of the lough continue to provide a safe habitat for a wide and varied range of wildlife, in fact Robert Brown states that "No comparative area in Europe has such a range of habitats supporting such luxuriant life".

The Lough itself continues to enthrall and occasionally frighten. When one watches the Galway Hookers and other yachts which glide over the surface on a sunny summer's afternoon the ancient Celtic name Cuan seems to be the most apt, but it is important to remember that the Vikings were also correct in their description of the Strang-fiord, with its whirlpools and strong tidal currents.

It has taken hundreds of millions of years to shape the lough, we must ensure that it remains a place of beauty and tranquillity.

Strangford

FERRY MOVING OUT INTO THE NARROWS

With Thanks to Down District Council

The People of the Lough

People have been living around Strangford Lough since the early Mesolithic period in 7000 B.C. That is almost 9000 years of human habitation.

The four Masters writing in the early 17th century said that the first inhabitant of Ireland was Cessair, Noah's granddaughter who arrived a few weeks before the flood and didn't survive the deluge. However there is no evidence for this other than in the imagination of the authors of early Christian manuscripts. There is, however, a great body of local archeological research which confirms that the earliest inhabitants were hunter gatherers who would have moved around the countryside in search of food, moving camp each time. There is evidence, that they ate wild boar and salmon as well as nuts and berries. They are thought to have come over from Scotland, arriving in small dugout canoes or boats. The Mesolithic period stretches for some three and a half thousand years during which time there was a marked development in the type of tools used. However it was still what we would think of as the Stone age and not particularly advanced.

The next wave of immigration was during the Neolithic period which started c.4000 B.C. There had been a gradual spread throughout Europe of a new style of living which was more sedentary and was based around farming and fixed settlements. Whereas elsewhere in Europe it is possible to argue that this was a gradual evolution among the Mesolithic communities, in Ireland the farmers must have moved to the Island. This is because they brought with them domestic animals such as goats, sheep and cattle, none of which were found naturally in Ireland. What the natives made of these strange beasts will remain a mystery. These early inhabitants left behind something other than their farm animals, their graves.

The Neolithic tombs were constructed from large stones and were a common form of burial in Europe (another indication that they were immigrants). Almost half of all the tombs which have been found in the British Isles are in Ireland. The one which is found in Audleystown is a double court tomb. Over 30 people were buried in its chambers which would imply that they were in constant use, an early form of family crypt.

The people

Archeologists have recovered various possessions from tombs such as decorated bowls. Other man-made structures left behind from this time are the stone circles which date from the end of the Neolithic period. Some, such as the one at the Giant's Ring outside Belfast, have a cairn in the middle, whereas the Five Sisters just outside Comber doesn't.

The Bronze age and Iron age which is dated by archeologists 2500-300B.C. and 300B.C.-400A.D. followed the late Neolithic period. This saw a rapid development of wealth in society with a corresponding development in technology. Again it is unclear as to whether or not this was due to a natural evolution in the sophistication of the local inhabitants, or because of a fresh wave of immigration. What is clear is that the people who were using the copper and tin, and later iron, to make weapons and implements had to import the raw materials as neither were found locally. It could be that there were established trade routes between the British Isles and the new technologies were simply imported. Given the very short distance between the eastern shores of Ulster and Scotland it is inconceivable that there was no trade between the two.

One of the problems about Irish history in this period is the lack of written evidence. We must work on the scant evidence which has been recovered both locally and in nearby Scotland. Despite the splendid work by generations of local archeologists, both professional and amateur, most of the evidence has been hidden or destroyed over the years.

What is clear is that the developments in technology resulted in a more structured form of society as individuals were able to accumulate wealth and, more importantly, defend it from would-be thieves. There was a gradual development in the sophistication of society and in the structure of settlements, from the two round houses thought to date from the Bronze Age, in Downpatrick, to the magnificent Iron Age fort at Navan.

With the growth in prosperity which accompanied the developments in technology so we see a corresponding growth in the number of weapons which can be dated to this period. There was an evolution from the long swords of the Bronze age to a shorter sword during the Iron age. At some time during the last millennium B.C. what had been small family settlements combined into tribes which had kings, usually the greatest warrior. These tribes fought each other to establish their own political boundaries. Each king had his own band of warriors who were young unmarried men in their late teens, a way of channelling the natural aggression of the young which has been used throughout the ages.

Towards the end of the Iron age information about the nature of the people becomes more accessible as in the first century A.D. the Romans invaded and then conquered what we refer to as England and parts of Wales. Although there is no firm evidence that they ever attempted to conquer Ireland they certainly considered it and so accumulated information about the island and its inhabitants. They told of a cold, damp land peopled by inhospitable and warlike savages. Significantly, given future Christian folklore, they also reported that there were no snakes. That the locals were warlike is confirmed by the tales of the great Ulster warriors such as CúChulainn, Fergus et al. These traditional heroes were constantly engaged in conflict with the fir-n-hErenn or 'men of Ireland'. Although these tales were recorded by later generations it is possible to surmise that they were in fact Iron age warriors.

By the 2nd century AD enough information had been accumulated to enable Ptolemy, the great Greek geographer, to compile a map of Ireland, despite the fact that he had never visited the country and was based in Alexandria in Egypt. The names of the people and rivers which he uses at first glance appear to be unfamiliar. However, they are remarkably close to the Gaelic names still used today and are merely a foreigner's attempt to translate the names they had heard, rather like a first former's attempt at French dictation.

No-one is sure when the Irish, as a separate tribal group arrived. In fact it is quite possible that such a group did not exist but instead that they gradually evolved out of the Celtic people who inhabited the country. The Celts certainly were widely spread throughout both the British Isles and parts of Europe. The Gaelic language is remarkably similar to other Celtic languages however by Roman times what is clear is that it was spoken by the people who lived in Ireland.

In the 5th century A.D. Ulstermen started to expand their own territory and invaded Scotland, the Isle of Man and parts of Wales. In Scotland there is evidence to suggest that there was an attempt at colonisation but in other areas they contented themselves with raids, snatching local people to bring back to Ireland as slaves. It was on one of these raids in Wales that they grabbed a young man who was to change their world completely. Patrick.

The people

According to tradition Patrick first arrived in Ireland as a slave and worked as a swineherd for Milcho at Slemish in Co. Antrim. He later escaped, returned to Wales, was converted to Christianity and decided to return to Ireland to convert Milcho, his former master. However instead of going to Co. Antrim he landed at Saul (perhaps an indication of poor navigation or divine intervention).

The author of the second life of St. Patrick (who is reputed to be the nephew of the saint) tells us that "He at length penetrated into a certain frith [thought to be the Slaney]. There, they concealed the bark, and they came a little distance into the country, that they might rest there and lie down; and there came upon them the swine-herd of a certain man of a good-natured disposition, though a heathen, whose name was Dichu, and who dwelt where now stands what is called Patrick's Barn [Saul]."

Patrick was accompanied by a group of clerics and after their first convert, Dichu, gave them the barn at Saul as a church, they were able to start their mission. It is unclear how quickly this was achieved. It is unwise to rely on the reports of the early monks as they were liable to exaggerate. However it is safe to say that given the warlike nature of the locals, the church became established within a surprisingly short time. It was the beginning of the end for the local pagan religion and provided the warring tribes with a common factor, although they did not suddenly become more peaceful and regional animosities still existed.

The church in Ireland became very strong and the monasteries which were founded round the shores of Strangford Lough by disciples of Patrick were to provide a strong base for Christianity at a time when it was under attack elsewhere in Europe. They became centres for learning and produced many of the earliest histories of Ireland as well as beautifully illustrated religious texts. The monks from these monasteries together with those from the nearby Bangor Abbey were responsible for the great missions to the rest of Europe in later centuries.

As the monasteries grew in significance so they accumulated great wealth. This was to prove their undoing centuries before Henry VIII thought of them as a source of income. Their reputation had spread far beyond the confines of Strangford and Ulster and in the 9th century they moved into the sights of the fearsome Norsemen.

The accounts about the Vikings come from their victims, the monks. As they were hardly going to be charitable to their attackers they tell of black-hearted murderers who committed every crime known to early Christian man. Ireland was unfortunate in that it came to the attention of the Vikings at a time when they had established permanent settlements elsewhere in the British Isles, most notably in the north of England. As they were reluctant to allow raids by their countrymen on their own territory the raiders had to look elsewhere and so they turned their attention on Ireland. Ulster would appear to have born the brunt of their attacks. They frequently raided the main ecclesiastical settlements, primarily because they knew from past experience elsewhere that this was where they were likely to find the best plunder.

The Vikings did establish some settlements in Ireland, most notably at Dublin and later at Strangford. Using Strangford as their base they launched attacks on Lough Erne, almost destroying Devenish. However perhaps their greatest unintentional effect was that they succeeded in uniting the various warring tribes together to fight them. In 926 Muircertach (son of Niall Glúndubh who had earlier united the tribes in the north of Ireland) actually defeated them in a sea battle on Strangford Lough. Unfortunately the unity was short lived and once the threat from the Vikings receded the various factions soon returned to attacking each other while nominally owing allegiance to a high king.

The monasteries never really recovered from the attacks of the Vikings and it took a new influx of settlers in the 12th century to re-establish some of the ancient sites. These new settlers were the Anglo-Normans.

The Normans had conquered England in the 11th century and there had been continuing contact between England and Ireland in the following years with trade flourishing between Dublin and Bristol. As the Norman kings extended and consolidated their control over England and later Wales, as well as their continental territories, so their attention began to turn westward. They were encouraged in this by their own leading churchmen. The church in Ireland was one of the last to come under the control of the Papacy and had held out longer than any other against the Gregorian reforms. The church was suspicious of the native church's ability to, or zeal for, reform. St. Bernard in his biography of Malachy of Armagh said of the Irish that "They were Christians in name, in fact pagans." In 1154 John of Salisbury (a close adviser of the Archbishop of Canterbury) got Pope Adrian IV to grant Ireland to Henry II. Shortly afterwards Norman barons (mostly from Wales) arrived in Ireland to establish the claim.

With regard to the area around Strangford the most important of these Anglo-Normans was John de Courcy. Despite almost all the Irish kings making submission to Henry, Anglo-Norman influence was confined for the most part to the eastern coast of Ireland. John de Courcy, originally from Somerset, started his 'conquest' of Ulster in 1177. One of the main subjects of his attentions was Lecale. The attack was unexpected and initially the local ruler Rory MacDonleavy fled. He later regrouped and returned with a large army and battle commenced on the banks of the Quoile. De Courcy won. Although Rory attacked de Courcy on a number of occasions he never recovered his kingdom.

John de Courcy had been accompanied by a number of knights who now wanted their reward. Among them was William, Baron Savage. Of all the new settlers his family was one of the few who succeeded in retaining most of its original estate through later upheavals. The Anglo-Normans had sacked Downpatrick and Armagh. All the clergy were captured and the lesser clergy killed. The relics and manuscripts belonging to the churches were seized. Once his control over the area had been firmly established, de Courcy started to build tower-houses and castles, the ruins of which we still see today.

In an attempt to atone for his murderous attacks on Downpatrick and Armagh he also started to endow the local churches. It was de Courcy who helped to re-establish Nendrum and Inch and built and endowed Downpatrick Cathedral. He later transferred what were thought to be the bodies of Patrick, Brigid and Colmcille to Downpatrick. His wife Affreca established the Cistercian monastery at Greyabbey. It is interesting to note, especially in light of the generally held poor opinion of the local clergy, that these new or revived establishments were usually 'staffed' with monks from England and France. They maintained close links with other monasteries of the same denomination thus, in theory, ensuring that the local church stayed within the control of the centralised church.

John de Courcy's marriage to Affreca (who was the daughter of Gottred, King of Man) gave him considerable power. He had access to a large fleet and he operated as if he was an independent ruler.

He minted his own currency and administered his own justice, both of which were supposed to be the prerogative of the King. For over 25 years de Courcy was left pretty much alone. In fact King John (he of Robin Hood fame or infamy) named him as his chief governor. However John was notoriously fickle with his favour and c.1200 he allowed Hugh de Lacy (from Meath) to wage war on de Courcy. After a vicious war conducted solely by the Anglo Normans, de Courcy was defeated and driven out of Ulster. On 29th May 1205 John created Hugh Earl of Ulster.

John's friendship with de Lacy was short lived. In 1210 William de Braose, Lord of Limerick incurred the King's displeasure and fled to stay with his kinsman de Lacy. Unfortunately for both de Braose and de Lacy, John happened to be in Ireland at the time. He was not alone as he had one of the largest armies ever raised at that time with him. He moved northwards to quell what was now a rebellion and on 16th July he was in Downpatrick. He soon laid siege to Carrickfergus Castle, where de Lacy and de Braose had taken refuge. In a very short time had succeeded in taking the castle, capturing about 30 knights and barons but not de Lacy and de Braose who had managed to escape. Two of the captured knights were William and Luke de Audley of Strangford.

Despite having been assisted by de Courcy, John decided that it would be prudent to keep the earldom of Ulster for himself. It can be argued that this was one of the high points of John's reign as he had proved himself to be victorious in battle and swift to punish any dissent. He received the allegiance of all his barons and also of the Irish chieftains. They remained loyal to him even when in 1215 his own 'English' barons forced him to sign the Magna Carta.

English rule continued with the Norman families holding the land together with powerful Irish families who had pragmatically accepted that they owed a nominal allegiance to the occupant of the English throne. The native Irish continued to till the land. They had never owned it so it mattered little who was in charge as their lives were pretty miserable whether the owner was a Norman or one of the Gaelic lords. Besides they had more important matters to worry about as the 14th century saw recurring famines and plagues, including the Black Death.

Ulster was one of the most independent of all the regions as it was sufficiently far away from the centre of government to make it more practical to allow the local landowners to get on with their own petty squabbles. Despite Ulster being taken over by the Scots under the command of Robert Bruce in the 14th century, there was little that the supposed government could do. In fact the Bruce got as far south as Dublin before being repulsed. The nominal rulers were too concerned with matters closer to hand in England and Scotland to bother much with their other territory and it was not until Tudor times that their attention once more wandered westward.

By 1485 when Henry Tudor defeated Richard III at Bosworth, one of the most powerful families in the Strangford area was the O'Neill family of Clanaboye. They were part of a larger clan who had a great influence on the history of Ulster. In 1449 Henry O'Neill recognised Henry VI as his liege lord. In return he won tacit recognition as overlord of Ulster with permission to attack all those who refused to submit to his rule. At the time this seemed like the sensible thing to do. Unfortunately he had backed the wrong side in the War of the Roses and when the Tudors came to power they were not favourably disposed to the O'Neills.

Henry VII did make attempts to re-establish his control over Ireland but he was more concerned with consolidating his power in England. His son Henry VIII was a different matter. He was not the first of the English kings to lay claim to Ireland but he was the first to determine to really rule it.

One of the most obvious effects that this had in Strangford was the dissolution of the monasteries in 1539. The break with Rome did not cause as much of an outcry as would at first be supposed. Despite the close links with the European church which had been established under de Courcy the church in Ireland had fallen back into its old ways. Celibacy was rare, the clergy took sides in the various disputes and in some cases were actively involved. The O'Neills were not convinced that it was worth making much of a fuss and anyway, initially, it didn't make that much of a difference. It was not until Henry's younger daughter Elizabeth came to the throne in 1558 that the effects of the reformation and counter-reformation started to take on any significance.

Whereas in England the Government was able to enforce its ban on priests, in Ireland they were unable to prevent them from returning to the country. These new priests were a different kettle of fish from the ones who had been expelled originally. They had been trained in Europe and were filled with all the fervour of missionaries and fired by the efforts being made at a counter-reformation. Of more significance, when Elizabeth and her ministers turned their attention to Ireland and decided that they should make more concerted efforts at settlement, the people who were sent to settle the land were protestant.

The original Anglo-Norman families had become fully assimilated over the centuries, marrying in to the local Gaelic families. Thus it was that when in 1562 Shane O'Neill (head of the O'Neill family) was summoned to Elizabeth's court to explain his actions during various attacks against the Earl of Sussex (her lord lieutenant) that he was accompanied by his cousin, the Earl of Kildare.

O'Neill struck an uneasy peace with Elizabeth but soon after his return to Ireland he was once more up to his old tricks and attacking local families. He attacked the MacDonnells of the Glens of Antrim, ostensibly to regain the Queen's favour. Whatever his professed intentions the end result was that he was the de facto ruler of Ulster. Elizabeth's lord deputy was Sir Henry Sidney who was determined to destroy Shane, however in the end it was his fellow countrymen who finally exacted their revenge for all his cruelty towards them. When his army was destroyed by the O'Donnells, Shane decided to take refuge with the MacDonnells to whom he himself had shown

no mercy. He was hacked to death during a feast.

It was after the death of Shane O'Neill that Elizabeth and her ministers hit on the idea of settling the country with Englishmen who would help to prevent the rise of another Shane. One of these settlers was Sir Thomas Smith who was vice-chancellor at Cambridge and a Privy councillor.

Sir Thomas and his son obtained letters patent to the lands of Clandeboye. This was despite the fact that Sir Brian MacPhelim O'Neill had fought against Shane O'Neill and had been knighted for his service for the crown. Smith made clear his intention to clear the land of all the native Irish, except for those who could be used to till the soil. Presumably Sir Brian was included. He didn't wait to find out. When Sir Thomas's son, Thomas landed at Strangford in August 1572 with approximately 100 fellow colonists, Sir Brian put a scorched earth policy into effect. He burnt and destroyed every building which might be used for shelter by the English - churches and abbeys were not spared. All of Thomas Smith's appeals for help to the new lord deputy, Sir William Fitzwilliam, fell on deaf ears as Fitzwilliam had been vehemently opposed to the expedition from the start. The hapless Smith was eventually murdered in Comber by his own Irish servants in 1573. Sir

Brian had an equally grisly end. He made his peace with the Earl of Essex (who had been granted most of Co. Antrim) and invited him to a feast in Belfast Castle. After three days of feasting the guests turned on their hosts and Sir Brian, his wife and his brother were all arrested. Their followers were immediately killed but Sir Brian, his wife and brother were sent to Dublin where they were hung, drawn and quartered.

The plantation of Ulster under Elizabeth was greeted by great resistance mainly from the Gaelic overlords. The O'Neills were seldom far away from the affray. Elizabeth should have been able to rely on the support of Hugh O'Neill if no-one else. His grandfather had been made Earl of Tyrone by the English and it was Elizabeth herself who had protected him from the murderous attentions of his uncle, Shane. He was brought up at court and educated as an Englishman and in 1585 had been proclaimed Earl of Tyrone.

Initially Hugh O'Neill lived up to the expectations of the Queen, however gradually he came to the realisation that while he may be powerful under the English patronage he could be even more powerful as a Gaelic King. He may or may not have been influenced by the fact that the English seemed as capable of capricious behaviour

as before, thinking nothing of inviting people to dine and then taking them hostage. There was also a more personal reason for his growing antagonism. In 1591 he had eloped with Mabel, the 20 year old sister of Sir Henry Bagenal (marshal of the army). Mabel died in 1596 and there is no evidence that she was an unwilling participant but Bagenal never forgave O'Neill although they continued to work together for a couple of years. In 1595 O'Neill rose in open rebellion backed by the other leading Gaelic families. For a long time the English were powerless to stop him and not even the 2nd Earl of Essex was able to crush the rebellion. O'Neill was eventually beaten in 1601 at Kinsale by Mountjoy. Elizabeth surprisingly offered O'Neill an effective pardon in 1603 whereby he renounced the title The O'Neill but held on to most of his lands. This was one of the last decisions the dying Elizabeth was to take. She was succeeded by James VI of Scotland.

It was under James that the real and lasting plantation of Ulster occurred and most of the new settlers were not English but Scottish. It is at this time that the last great changes in land ownership occurred around Strangford Lough.

When James inherited the throne the main landowners around the lough were the Earl of

Kildare who owned most of Lecale, the Savages who owned Upper Ards and Con O'Neill of Clanaboye who owned the rest.

At the end of the Nine Years War Con O'Neill was imprisoned at Carrickfergus Castle accused of making war against Elizabeth. This was rather unfair as it was really a dispute about some wine. O'Neill had been dining at Belfast Castle and had sent his servants off to get some more wine from a nearby cellar. They returned sometime later without the wine, it having been 'confiscated' by some soldiers. On hearing their tale he sent his own soldiers out to recover the wine. They succeeded in their task but several soldiers were killed and O'Neill arrested. This came to the attention of Hugh Montgomery who was the 6th Laird of Braidstone and a friend of the new king. He devised a plan whereby he could rescue O'Neill and help himself to greater glory.

He sent his agent over to Carrickfergus where he set about wooing the daughter of O'Neill's gaoler. After a couple of days (and nights) he succeeded in persuading her to open O'Neill's cell. O'Neill shinned down a rope into a waiting boat and made his escape. Once safely in Scotland O'Neill promised to divide his estate with Montgomery if he would ask the new King for a pardon. In the event he ended up dividing his estate in three as James Hamilton insisted on being cut in on the deal. Con who knew what the land was like readily agreed to give up the North Down and Ards while he kept almost half of his estate centred on Castlereagh. Both Hamilton and Montgomery had worked as secret agents for James and he was as keen as they were to extend their influence into Ireland. The deal was made in April 1605.

The reason why Con was quite happy with the arrangement, apart from the obvious benefit of receiving a royal pardon, was that he knew that the territory which he had given away had not been restored after his ancestor Sir Brian MacPhelim O'Neill had burnt everything during Thomas Smith's ill-fated attempts at colonisation over 50 years before. There were very few people left on the land and anyone who wanted to settle it was going to have to spend a lot of money just to make the place habitable let alone profitable.

In the 16th century Angus of Saltires had said that "the Ardes of Uladh, scarce and starving, is a country without happiness and without religion". The Scottish settlers who arrived over with Hamilton and Montgomery in the early 1600s were not going to argue with this assessment. The author of the Montgomery Manuscript reported that "30 cabins could not be found, nor any stone walls, but ruined roofless churches... and a stump of an old castle in Newtown, in each of which some Gentlemen sheltered themselves at their first coming over."

The new arrivals found that they had to import everything from labour to raw materials with which to construct their houses. At Newtownards even Sir Hugh and his family had to make do initially. "In Summer 1608, some of the priory walls were roofed and fitted for his [Sir Hugh's] lady and children and servants (which were many) to live in" (M.M)

Montgomery built a harbour at Donaghadee, just a short sea journey from Portpatrick and a flood of settlers began to arrive, each bringing a cow and a few sheep. Lady Montgomery ordered that watermills be erected in each parish to grind corn and the soil fertilised with kelp.

The Montgomery manuscripts report a positive utopia after only two years. "Now everybody minded their trades, and the plough, and the spade, building and setting fruit trees in orchards and gardens and by ditching in their grounds. The old women spun and the young girls plied their nimble fingers at knitting and everybody was innocently busy. Now the golden peaceable age renewed, no strife, contention, querulous lawyers, or Scottish or Irish feuds, between clanns and families, and sirnames, disturbing the tranquillity of those times."

Given the outbreaks of violence which greeted attempts at plantation elsewhere in Ireland the settlement around the Strangford Lough area was remarkably free from tension. One reason may be that in the early stages of settlement, under the Anglo-Normans, the lives of the peasants didn't change much. Also there was another factor absent elsewhere: the land had been devastated by the Gaelic overlord and for the most part depopulated – there were no displacements, and no one felt that their land had been stolen from them. For the most part the major landowners were very tolerant of the religious beliefs of their Irish tenants. Rev. James O'Laverty tells of them hiding priests and, when the penal laws were at their height, of registering their tenants under suitably protestant sounding names.

This is not to say that there were no tensions. Certainly the introduction of settlers who were of a different religious denomination was bound to heighten fears on both sides at times of strife elsewhere in the country. During the 1641 rebellion local old-Irish (that is Anglo-Norman) landlords did become involved and ended up forfeiting their estates. The newcomers, Montgomery and Hamilton, helped to defend Lisburn when it came under attack from the rebels and as news of massacres spread so did fear and mistrust. When Munro landed at Carrickfergus in April 1642 the new Scottish settlers were eager recruits. At one battle Hugh Montgomery, the grandson of the original Montgomery, was captured by the Irish.

The situation in Ireland was further confused at this time by the English Civil War which was raging across the sea. The various factions couldn't make up their minds who to support. In the event it didn't much matter who they fought for during the rebellion when Cromwell arrived in Ireland in 1649. Both Montgomery and Hamilton were royalists, as were most of the Scottish settlers (the English were after all the auld enemy) and they raised an army to oppose the parliamentary forces. At a battle near Lisburn they were completely defeated by the parliamentary army. Montgomery and Hamilton forfeited their estates as did other Gaelic landlords, although both were restored after the Restoration.

The 17th century was one of rebellion and unrest in Ireland in general. As the colonisation of the island continued apace with the crushing of the Gaelic landlords, so the sectarian divides became more rigid and acquired the weight of the law. Most significantly in the Strangford area the settlers who were members of the Presbyterian church found that they were being punished for the sins of the parliamentarians and that the laws which began to be introduced placing restrictions on religious freedom applied as much to them as to their Catholic neighbours. This led to a development of mistrust of authority which was to have great significance a century later.

The Williamite Wars certainly raised religious tensions in the area. The population was again gripped with fears of massacre and thus many people in the area were willing recruits when Schomberg's army landed in Bangor. In the event, for the population as a whole the success of the protestant William was to make little change in their lives. If anything in respect of the so-called penal laws things got worse as they were debarred from political involvement as well as all the other petty restrictions on inheritance and bearing of arms and ownership of horses etc. The so-called Test Act of 1704 said that anyone who wanted to hold public office (including joining either the army or a militia) had to produce written proof that they were communicant members of the established Church. Although the Toleration Act gave them some relief one of their main grievances concerned their clergy.

There was a high degree of absenteeism amongst the anglican clergy who often held several livings (or parishes) and were either unwilling or unable to minister to them all. In Ulster this gap in pastoral care was seen as an opportunity for expansion and presbyterianism made great inroads into the local anglican population. Realising the danger, the anglican clergy began to harry the ministers. Indeed Swift thought that they were more dangerous than "the papists". Another constant source of irritation was the legal obligation to pay tithes to the anglican ministers. Much more annoying and humiliating than the continued harassment of their clergy, however, was the failure of the state to recognise the validity of their marriages.

Despite this in a country which lived under almost constant fear of 'papish revolt' for the most part the various restrictions were not strictly adhered to. It would not do to completely alienate your potential allies and in the second half of the century The Patriot Party, under the leadership of Henry Grattan, were committed to the repeal of the penal law and universal emancipation.

The first half of the 18th century saw a period of great want. There were a series of crop failures and plagues and the spectre of famine stalked the land. It is thought that the number of people who died during this famine was comparable to the number who died in the Great Famine of the mid-19th century. Although they were also affected the presbyterians did have an escape route, not just across to Scotland but further afield. There was a dramatic increase in the number of immigrants to the American colonies at this time. The would-be immigrants went for a variety of reasons, not least of which was the promise of a better life which was held out as a lure. These settlers were to have a profound influence on events in their new land.

Towards the end of the century there were two major developments elsewhere in the world which were to have a dramatic effect on life in Ulster. The first was the American War of Independence which began with the Declaration of Independence on 4th July 1776. Although the government in Dublin was horrified by this revolt against the crown, the population of Ulster, especially the eastern counties, were very interested. Their sympathies were with the rebels, many of whom were emigrants from Ulster. The Belfast Newsletter carried daily reports from the colonies, recognising the desire for information amongst its readers. However in 1778 France, the traditional enemy, joined the war on the side of the rebels. In April of the same year Paul Jones sailed his ship 'Ranger' into Belfast Lough and attacked and seized 'Drake', a Royal Navy vessel based there. This raised the spectre of invasion by a foreign power. The establishment were horrified and quickly called for Volunteers. They flooded in.

The threat of invasion was never very great but there was a greater threat from within. The country was rapidly emptied of regular troops who were dispatched to fight in the colonies, so a large militia, which was armed locally, would prove a useful deterrent to anyone who wanted to take advantage of the situation. The Volunteers were to prove a useful tool for the Patriot Party who wanted greater autonomy for the Dublin Parliament. Grattan referred to them as "the armed property of the nation". He and his party were committed to gradual reform, however their commitment was treated with suspicion by radicals in the north. They were inspired by the ideals set forward by the other great event in the closing decades of the 18th century – the French Revolution

Again the Belfast Newsletter carried daily reports from France. The Belfast Volunteers sent a message of support to Paris. The French Revolution and its ideals of brotherhood, liberty and freedom struck a chord, especially among the radicals in Belfast. The 18th century was the age of enlightenment and one of the leading centres for the new ideas were the Scottish universities. The presbyterians in Ulster were forbidden, by law, from attending Trinity University in Dublin and so anyone wanting to get a university education went to Scotland. This was especially true of the presbyterian clergy. They were not allowed to be trained locally and so had to go to either Glasgow or Edinburgh. Here they got caught up with all the new radical ideas.

The United Irishmen were formed in 1791 in Belfast. Initially they were tolerated by the authorities. They ran their own newspaper, the Northern Star, which concentrated on local news and was soon attracting articles by some of the leading radicals, amongst them Rev. James Porter of Greyabbey and Rev. William Steele Dickson from Ballyhalbert. The involvement of the presbyterian clergy was crucial in the support which the movement was able to attract in the eastern counties of Ulster. Elsewhere in Ulster the local population was roughly 50-50 but in both Antrim and Down there was a very marked protestant majority. In fact in certain areas the population was almost 100% protestant. They could therefore afford to be more tolerant of new ideas and in fact the presbyterian communities were very active champions of local catholics. It was the presbyterian community in Belfast who paid for the erection of the first Catholic church in the town. Elsewhere in Ulster the situation was not so relaxed. Secret societies such as the Peep-o-day boys (protestant) and the Defenders (catholic) were constantly engaging in skirmishes. This came to a head in 1795 at the battle of the Diamond in Loughgall. This was to lead to the founding of the Orange Order.

The 1798 rising was to split the countryside around Strangford. It pitted family members against each other and landlord against tenant. The United Irishmen were particularly well supported in the Ards peninsula, which was also home to their chief opponent Lord Castlereagh who lived at Mount Stewart. He was ruthless in crushing the revolt elsewhere in Ireland, but in Strangford it became a personal matter. He personally led the hunt for members of his own tenancy who had been involved. No-one escaped. Many were captured and deported, some were executed including James Porter, the presbyterian minister for Greyabbey. The rising was crushed and its only lasting effect was to hasten the political union between Ireland and the rest of Great Britain which happened in 1801.

It was during the 18th century that Ulster began to develop an industry which was to lead to it going from the poorest province in Ireland at the end of the 17th century to the richest by the mid-19th century. The industry was Linen.

Up until this point the economy of Ulster was almost completely rural. This laid it open to great danger as was seen at the beginning of the century. Linen had always been produced in Ireland. The fertile countryside and good irrigation made the growing and processing of flax relatively easy. The influx of Huguenot refugees into the province in the early decades of the century, who had great textile skills, helped in the development of the industry. Initially it was run on a very small scale. Farmers were able to augment their income by weaving their own cloth and selling it at market. Nearly every market town had a linen hall and trade was encouraged and assisted by developments in communications. The Newry Canal was opened in 1742, the ports of Donaghadee and Belfast were thriving and, more importantly, there was a period of relative peace which helped the development of economic prosperity.

Initially the production of linen was done on a purely piecemeal basis by individual farmers. The linen merchants bought the cloth unbleached which gave the farmers a quick return for their money. However the developments in industrial production soon led to the formation of mills. These were not confined just to Belfast, although there was a large concentration of them there. The main requirement for a linen mill was a ready source of water and mills grew up in Comber, Newtownards, Killyleagh and Downpatrick. Throughout the 19th century the linen industry grew and as it did so did the prosperity of the local community.

There were still natural disasters such as the famine which raged in the 1840s. It is commonly believed that the famine didn't affect the eastern counties of Ulster. In fact the potato blight had first appeared in Co. Antrim and the Ards peninsula was badly hit. The people in the area were very badly affected as it coincided with an economic decline in the area as handloom weavers were finding it increasingly difficult to compete with the technological developments in the industry. However the effects were mitigated to a certain extent by the system of land tenure in Ulster which differed significantly from elsewhere in Ireland and gave the tenant farmers more security. There was not the same level of subsistence farming and so there was a greater range of crops. Also nowhere was too far away from the sea.

Emigration continued apace with advertisements appearing in local newspapers offering great new opportunities in the colonies and of course England and America continued to lure people away. For those who chose to remain there were the traditional industries of fishing and farming. Women in the area were able to augment the family's income by doing 'sprigging' or 'flowering' on muslin or linen. Mr. and Mrs. S. C. Hall writing in 1846 said that "Through the whole of this district - the barony of Ards and that of Castlereagh - a large proportion of the peasantry are employed in what is technically termed 'flowering' - embroidering muslin chiefly for the Glasgow manufacturer, material and pay fixed sums for the workmanship. The workers earn generally about 3 shillings a week, a small sum, but as the majority of the inmates of a cottage are similarly employed sufficient is obtained to procure the necessities of life; and indeed some of its luxuries for the interiors of many of the cabins present all aspects of cheerfulness and comfort." That this cottage industry continued to be an important source of income is born out by a couple of advertisements which appeared in the Newtownards Chronicle in 1910. One was from a John Cully who was an agent for a linen firm for special sewers who could do monograms and crest work . The agent offered constant work and high wages.

The people

The other advert was for an agent it wanted; "Capable agents to give out handkerchiefs for embroidery: the goods are well paid and provide pleasant and remunerative occupation for young women in their homes, liberal commission paid to agents".

Although the life of the average worker was still rather ghastly there was an overall rise in the general prosperity. The advances in transport, namely the railway, not only helped trade in the area but also provided an alternative source of employment. The growth of the large towns provided an alternative to emigration and the growth in shipbuilding in the 19th century and the exciting new world of airplane construction in the early 20th century, offered young men new opportunities.

There were still political tensions. The growth in the Home Rule movement once more raised the spectre of sectarian strife and once more caused neighbour to look with suspicion on neighbour. It is ironic that the descendants of the United Irishmen from a century earlier were amongst the most vociferous supporters of the Union. Once more Volunteer movements sprang up and at one stage there was a very real threat of civil war. The intervention of the First World War averted this although it was to have a devastating effect on the local population.

Every town and village around Strangford Lough lost many of their young men on the fields of France. The war memorials in the towns make depressing reading with families losing their sons, in some cases more than one. Many acts of bravery achieved official recognition. Many more did not.

Some aspects of life around the Lough remain unchanged. Although technological advances have meant that the lives of the inhabitants have become a lot easier than it was for their forefathers, the land and the sea continue to provide employment as well as enjoyment for many.

A brief history of the Strangford area spanning 9000 years has of necessity to be sketchy. However what comes across from any study of the area is the resilience of the population. From earliest times they have withstood many trials and tribulations and have come out reasonably intact.

The Lough itself has influenced the lives of the people to a great extent. It has been the source of their prosperity and also a source of danger, both man-made and natural. A walk along its shores reveals evidence of all the past generations from the Neolithic standing stones at Comber, through the ruins of the early Christian monasteries, the Anglo-Norman tower-houses, the large stately homes of the 18th and 19th centuries, the homes of the ordinary people to the modern developments of the 20th century. A glance at the names of the local population reveal names dating from the 12th century onwards, Savages, Nugents, Hamiltons and Montgomerys have all left their mark on what today remains an area of outstanding natural beauty. Long may it continue to be so.

Bibliography

Barton, J., *A history of Ulster* (Belfast, 1992)

Bassett, G. H. *County Down guide and directory* (Dublin, 1886; reprint, Belfast 1988)

Bell, P., Brett, C., and Matthews, R. *Portaferry and Strangford* U.A.H.S., (Belfast, 1969)

Bence-Jones, M., *A guide to Irish Country Houses* (London, 1978, reprinted London, 1988)

Blaney, J., *18th Century wrecks around the Upper Ards* in Upper Ards Historical Journal Vol 13 (1989)

Brett, C.E.B., *Court houses and Market houses of the Province of Ulster* (Belfast, 1973)

Brownlow, W.S., *The Brownlows* in Upper Ards Historical Journal Vol 2.(1978)

ed. Day, A., *Letters from Georgian Ireland* (Belfast, 1991)

Denvir, R., *The ferry boat disaster of 1947* in Upper Ards Historical Journal Vol 18 (1994)

Gilmore, J.J., *Lisbane Church* in Upper Ards Historical Journal Vol 11 (1987)

Green, E.R.R. *The industrial archaeology of County Down* H.M.S.O. (Belfast 1963)

Harris, W. *Ancient and present state of County of Down* (Dublin, 1744)

Hayward, R., *In praise of Ulster* (Belfast, 1938)

Hughes, A.J., and Hannan, R.J., *Place-names of Northern Ireland Vol. 2 The Ards* (Belfast, 1992)

Lewis, S., *Topographical dictionary of Ireland* (2nd edition, Dublin, 1875)

Mallory, J.P., and McNeill, T.E., *The archaeology of Ulster* (Belfast, 1991)

Magee, J., *A journey through Lecale* (Belfast, 1991)

Montgomery, W., *Montgomery Manuscripts: colonisation of the Ards* (Belfast, 1830)

O'Laverty, J. *The dioceses of Down and Connor* (Dublin, 1878)

Rowan-Hamilton, Lt-Col D.A., *The Hamiltons of Killyleagh* in The Dufferin Chronicles Vol. 1

Stevenson, J. *Two centuries of life in Down* (Belfast, 1920, reprint, Belfast 1990)

Stewart, A.T.Q., *The summer soldiers* (Belfast, 1995)

Young, R.M., *Belfast and the Province of Ulster* (Brighton, 1909)

Author's Acknowledgements

I would like to thank the following people who helped me during the research for this book. Sally Skilling of the Ulster Folk and Transport Museum; the staff of the Linen Hall Library, Belfast; the staff of the Bangor Public Library; the staff of the Newtownards Public Library; Lesley Simpson of the Down County Museum; John McKenna of Saltwater Brig; Fred Warden of Cunningburn Mill and everyone else who gave me nuggets of information or pointed me in the correct direction.

Local directory
and Sponsors

Cottage Publications would like to express their sincere thanks
to the following businesses and organisations without whose
help and support this book would not have been possible.

NAME AND ADDRESS	TEL	FAX
Art Gallery		
Charles Gilmore Galleries, 31 Church Road, Holywood	01232 428555	
Builders		
McGimpsey & Kane, 15A Rowreagh Road, Kircubbin	012477 38646	012477 38832
Chiropractor		
Andrew Noble, Chiropractic Clinic, 19 Hamilton Road, Bangor	01247 471200	
Coffee Merchant		
Johnson Brothers (Belfast) Ltd., 137 Hillsborough Old Road, Lisburn	01846 679121	01846 668800
Conservation Charity		
The National Trust, Rowallane House, Saintfield, Ballynahinch	01238 510721	01238 511242
Mount Stewart House and Gardens	012477 88387	
Castle Ward	01396 881204	
Craft Shop		
Ards Crafts, 31 Regent Street, Newtownards	01247 826846	

NAME AND ADDRESS	TEL	FAX
Decorative Items for Interiors		
Rara Avis, 12 Main Street, Greyabbey	012477 88300	012477 88300
Equestrian Academy		
Peninsula Equestrian Academy, 4 Cardy Road, Greyabbey	012477 88681	012477 88681
Estate Agents / Chartered Surveyors		
Alexander Reid & Frazer, 6 English Street, Downpatrick	01396 612821	01396 612815
Framing and Gallery		
Sheldon Gallery, 15 Mill Street, Newtownards	01247 812526	01247 812526
Freelance Writing and Editing		
Jane Crosbie, Bangor	01247 460064	
Guesthouse Accommodation and Residential Course Venue		
The Narrows, 8 Shore Road, Portaferry	012477 28148	012477 28105
Hoops Courtyard		
Traders at Hoops Courtyard, Main Street, Greyabbey	012477 88541	
Including: Archway Antiques; Encore Exclusive Nearly New Boutique; Hoops Coffee Shop; Hoops Toys and Gifts; John Dunlop Gallery; Noah Noah; Pat Bradford Antiques and Bric-a-Brac; The Irvine Gallery		
Ice-Cream Parlour & Coffee Shop		
Dolley Madisons, 1-3 Castle Street, Portaferry	012477 28555	
Inn & Restaurant		
The Old Schoolhouse Inn, 100 Ballydrain Road, Comber	01238 541182	01238 542583
The Saltwater Brig, Rowreagh Rd, Kircubbin (Main Portaferry Road)	012477 38797	

NAME AND ADDRESS	TEL	FAX
Insurance Brokers		
Spratt Insurance, 16-18 Mill Street, Newtownards	01247 813019	01247 812084
Irish Crafts, Coffee Shop and Art Gallery		
The Harlequin/The Bridge Gallery, Castle Street, Portaferry	012477 29675	
Local Authority		
Ards Borough Council, Tourist Information Centre 31 Regent Street, Newtownards	01247 826846	
Down District Council, Tourist Information Centre, 74 Market Street, Downpatrick	01396 612233	01396 612350
Newsagents & Booksellers		
Page 1 Books & News, 7 Regent Street, Newtownards	01247 813072	01247 820978
Restaurant & Pub		
The Smuggler's Table, The Harbour, Killyleagh	01396 828778	01396 828036
Restaurant		
The Cornstore, 2-8 Castle Street, Portaferry	012477 29779	
Sports Goods & Trophies		
In-Sport, 15 Frances Street, Newtownards	01247 813811	01247 813811
Traditional Paint Specialists		
Sloane's Emporium, 8-10 Shore Street, Killyleagh	01396 821089	

Dear Reader

We hope you have found this book both enjoyable and useful. If you feel that it could have been improved in any way do please let us know. This is just one of our range of illustrated titles. Other towns and areas currently featured include:–

Ballycastle and the Heart of the Glens
Ballymena
Ballymoney
Banbridge
Bangor
City of Derry
Coleraine and the Causeway Coast
Donaghadee
Hillsborough
Holywood
Larne and the Road to the Glens
Lisburn
Newry
Newtownards

If you require any further information please call or fax us on (01247) 883876, E-Mail us on cottage_publ@online.rednet.co.uk or write to:–

Cottage Publications
15 Ballyhay Road
Donaghadee, Co. Down
N. Ireland, BT21 0NG